Sometimes, No Means I Love You

Written by
Kessa Scott

Illustrated by
Poornima Madhushani

Dedicated to my zesty daughter
Clara Joy.
May your spirit always sparkle as
brightly as it does now.

Sometimes you hear "Yes," and it's sunshine and rainbows.

Sometimes you hear "No," and it's a little bit tricky. Why?

When I say no, I'm saying:
"There's a better way."

When you hear no, you think:
"Why can't I have one more?"

When I say no, I'm saying: "Healthy food helps us grow strong."

When I say no, I'm saying:
"Rest will help you feel your best."

When I say no, I'm saying:
"Patience can be a treasure."

When you hear no, you think:
"I don't want to stop!"

When I say no, I'm saying:
"There is more to experience and discover."

When you hear no, you think:
"Why won't you help me?"

When I say no, I don't mean to ruin your day or limit your fun.

When I say no,
it's for a reason.

To guide and protect you.

But more than anything...
When I say no, what I'm
really saying is:

"I LOVE YOU."

Visit my website for free downloadables and to join my email list for updates!

If you enjoyed the story, please consider leaving a review. Your feedback helps other readers discover this book and makes a big difference for independent authors like me.

Check out the Sometimes, No Means I Love You Series for more fun, including an engaging companion Workbook!

Made in the USA
Las Vegas, NV
12 December 2024